Ghost Tales from the Historical Archives

Scottish Paranormal

Book 2

This book is written in British English

ISBN: 9798850540586

First Published 2023

Contents

The Curious Case of Ballechin House

Ballechin House in Perthshire was built in 1806 for the Stuart family. The substantial property stood on the site of a manor house occupied by successive generations of the family for over 300 years. In the same year of completion, Robert Stuart was born in the house. Robert stayed there until he was 19, when he travelled to India to work with the East Indian Company. He also served in the army, reaching the rank of Major. He inherited Ballechin House in 1834, yet did not return until 1850, instead opting to let the house to tenants.

When he did return, he stayed in a small cottage in the grounds until the lease expired and he moved back into the main house. He was considered by the local community to be strange and eccentric. He was a highly successful man yet lived in a small cottage, and his religious beliefs had very much been influenced by his time in India, with him developing a strong belief in reincarnation, something that was largely dismissed within the Christian community.

He did not enjoy being in the company of other people, and lived at the large mansion alone, until he eventually employed a local farmers daughter, named Sarah, as a housekeeper to help in his later years. His only other company were his 14 spaniels, and he openly vowed that when he died he would reincarnate in the body of his favourite spaniel.

In 1873, Sarah died of an unknown illness. Much mystery surrounded her passing, she was only 27 years old, and the rumour was she had been found dead in Major Stuart's bed rather than in the servant's quarters. The following year, Major Stuart died, and was buried next to Sarah. The property was inherited by John Stuart, Major

Stuart's nephew, and as a devout Roman Catholic, he set about righting what he saw as his uncle's wrongs. He had all the remaining dogs at the house shot, starting with his uncle's favourite, and had the cottage in the grounds converted to a retreat for nuns, in recognition of his sister, Isabella, who was a nun.

Shortly after taking up residency in the house, John's wife reported smelling dogs in the study. As this had been the study used by Robert, she thought it was simply a lingering odour from his dogs from when he had been there, but when she was opening the window, she felt a distinct nudge against her leg, which she described as being just like a dog. The house was searched, but no dogs were found.

Over the next few days, she heard knocking noises from various parts of the house, gunfire and raised voices, as though people were arguing, although she could not make out what was being said. A priest, Father Hayden, who stayed at the house reported hearing a sound like a dog nudging at his bedroom door trying to get in at night, yet when he checked there was nothing there. He also heard loud screaming.

By the late 1870's, the activity had increased to the level that one of the senior house staff could take no more, and she moved out. She later met Father Hayden by chance, and when they were discussing their experiences at the house, she revealed to him that the room in which he had slept had been Major Stuart's bedroom.

In 1895, while John Stuart was discussing business with his associates in the former Major's study, they were interrupted by 3 loud bangs on the wall, which all reported sounded as though they came from within the room. This was later said to have been a death warning, as shortly after John was hit and killed in a freak accident when he was hit by a cab in London.

The house and estate were passed to John Stuart, and leased to a family for a year, yet the only stayed for 11 weeks. When they left, willingly forfeiting the advance rent they had paid, they claimed that during the short time they had stayed there they experienced the same knocking noises throughout the house, and of hearing people arguing. The full formed phantom figure of a woman in what they described as being a silk dress was also seen on several occasions, and at other times the sound of a silk dress trailing along the wooden floors of the corridors was heard.

One of the daughters had been so terrified one night by the sound of limping footsteps around her bedroom that her screams brought her family running to her. They too all heard the footsteps. It was later revealed that the room was Major Stuart's bedroom, with unconfirmed reports that he had suffered a leg injury during his time in India and walked with a limp. Yet this was not the only bedroom where unexplained phenomena was happening, with other family members saying they were awoken by the bed covers being pulled from them.

With Ballechin House standing empty, and no-one willing to take up a lease on it due to its haunted reputation, it soon attracted the attention of Paranormal Researchers, including John Crichton-Stuart, the 3rd Marquess of Bute. He had a keen interest in the Paranormal and was friendly with Fredrick Myers, founder of the Society for Psychical Research, and Ada Freer, a psychic medium who was also a member of the Society. In 1896 he, along with Ada who went under her pseudonym Miss X, started an investigation at the house, aided by other members of the society, a total of 35 people.

During the investigation, the apparition of a nun was reported, and a later Ouija board session gave the name of the nun as 'Ishbel,' which was noted as being very close to the name of John Stuart's sister, whom he had converted the cottage in the estate to a nun's retreat for. Ada Freer reported seeing the nun's face, which she said had white eyes and a pained look.

Freer later claimed to have seen Ishbel appear in the grounds, along with another spirit that she named Margot, and to also see a woman in the drawing room with a 'coarsely handsome face.' The nun was reported on several occasions by different members of the investigation team.

Other members of the investigation reported hearing a quiet conversation between women in the grounds, possibly Ishbel and Margot, and the Reverend Charles Shaw heard a loud groan while in his bedroom, as he looked to see where it had come from, he had a flashing vision of a crucifix on the wall. Footsteps were heard throughout the house from unoccupied areas, sometimes reported as shuffling footsteps. It is possible this description could relate to either the 'swishing' of the reported spirit with the silk dress previously seen, or the limping footsteps of Major Stuart.

On one occasion, the witnesses went to see where the footsteps were coming from and upon arrival saw a door close to one of the bedrooms. They checked, and the room was empty. Reports of hearing the arguing voices were also made, although this time it was clarified as being a male and a female voice, possibly Major Stuart and is former housekeeper, Sarah.

Banging and knocks were also reported throughout the

period of the investigation, with some being woken up by someone knocking at their door, only to find the corridor outside empty and quiet. There were also reports of hearing a group of people running along the corridors.

On the anniversary of the Major's death, Ada Freer and 2 investigators, Miss Langton and one identified only as Mr T, decided to eat in the room the Major had used as a lounge. Before they ate, Anna Freer reported seeing 2 dogs, 1 which she identified as a spaniel, and after dinner as they sat playing games, all 3 heard heavy footsteps walking down the corridor, into the room and past them before fading. They also heard the sound of a man and woman arguing in the corridor several times, yet every time when they checked, there was no one there.

 Later in the night, before going to bed, the sound of the heavy footsteps were heard again, starting from where they had stopped earlier, and walking back past them, out of the room and down the corridor. Miss Langton recorded in her diary that after she had gone to bed that night, she was woken by the sound of footsteps coming down the corridor, but quieter this time, she suggests it was someone wearing slippers. They stopped at her door, and she again heard a man and woman argue, yet as soon as she opened her door everything fell silent, and the corridor was empty.

Despite the evidence gathered, and with both publishing their findings, neither Lord Bute nor Ada Freer came to any conclusion on the reported haunting at Ballechin House. Another member of the Society for Psychical Research subsequently leased the property in secret, and reported no activity during his stay and disputed any of the claims made by Lord Bute and Ada Freer. Despite Lord Bute becoming vice president of the Society, a subsequent fall out with other members saw the Society distance themselves from having any connection with the reports of the hauntings.

Ballechin House remained unoccupied, and in 1932 was considered to be in such poor condition that it was deemed uninhabitable. In 1963, after a fire left only the servants' quarters and the outhouse intact, the property was completely demolished. Yet the memory of the house lives on. In 2019, the interior was created as a temporary museum display in Perth, complete with ringing phones, and lighting and sound effects to give visitors an idea of the atmosphere of the house. As for the site of the actual house, reports of a black spaniel seen roaming the area before disappearing are still made.

The Battle of Culloden

On 16th April, 1746, the Battle of Culloden was fought, marking the final stand of the 1745 Jacobite Rebellion and the last field battle ever fought on British soil.

The view across Culloden Battle Field

The 1745 was the final uprising to restore the Stuart monarchy to the British throne, with the forces being led by Charles Edward Stuart, better known as Bonnie Prince Charlie, or the Young Pretender. Having landed in Scotland from France in July, 1745, Charles raised substantial support for his cause, primarily through the Highlands of Scotland, although he had support across the Lowlands and in England also.

His forces were swift and efficient, taking Perth on 4th September, 1745, Edinburgh on 17th September and Carlisle on November 15th. He continued south, until he reached Derby, just 130 miles from his final goal of London, on 4th December, where he paused prior to making his next move. He had been promised the support of French and English Jacobites, but they had not yet arrived.

Charles was influenced by concerns raised, primarily by Lord George Murray, and against his own judgement, Charles felt he had no option but to agree to retreating due to the growing concern. This was a disastrous decision. Unknown to Prince Charles and his commanders, the Welsh Jacobites had risen in support of his campaign, and the London authorities were in a panic over the advancement of his army, and preparations were being made to take King George II to the European Continent for his own safety.

His march back was not an easy one. The Government forces had re-taken much of the territory while his army had been moving south, yet he was again largely victorious, reaching Stirling in January 1746. Morale within his troops was however wavering at this point. The Highland armies traditionally did not do battle in winter, due to the harsh weather conditions they faced. Although still in the Lowlands, several of the Highland Commanders wanted to return to their homelands for the rest of the winter months.

A failed attempt to take Stirling castle, which was little more than a token gesture, did little to boost morale. Canons that had to be man-handled and hoisted up sheer cliff faces were destroyed in the first few shots from the castle canons. By February, Prince Charles had decided to take his forces back to the Highlands, pursued by the Duke of Cumberland, and a large government army.

By Spring, 1746, the Jacobites had re-taken Inverness and established it as a stronghold, yet the Duke of Cumberland was not far away, having taken Aberdeen. With funds and morale within the Jacobite forces continuing to waver, it was inevitable the two forces would meet in battle sooner rather than later. Three sites were scouted by the Jacobite commanders as potential locations. A location around 1km away from the final battlefield was the best of the three, however, fate was to deliver another blow to the Jacobite cause.

The Duke of Cumberland's forces had set up camp in Nairn, less than 15 miles from the Jacobite Head Quarters at Culloden House. On 15th April, a night-time attack was launched by the Jacobites, however, by dawn they had not yet reached the Government camp, and so retreated to Culloden House. After the exhausting night-time march, most of the Jacobite forces were resting when they received word that the Duke of Cumberland had mobilised his army.

Prince Charles and his commanders formed their army at Drumossie Moor, to protect the road to Inverness. This was far from an ideal site, and one which Prince Charles had been advised against using due to the marshy ground not suiting the Highlanders charge tactics, yet it ultimately became the battlefield.

Faced with a larger army and with weather conditions causing poor visibility, the Jacobite forces came under fire from the Duke of Cumberland's artillery. Prince Charles held, waiting for his opponents to make the first move onto the battlefield, yet with that not coming, he eventually ordered his men to charge. Cumberland's forces continued to fire, slaughtering the charging Jacobites.

With rebellions within the Jacobite army and them being out gunned and out flanked by the Government forces resulting in a blood-bath, they retreated. The battle lasted just 40 minutes, yet around 2,000 of the estimated 5,000-6,000 Jacobite army were killed, compared to just 300 of the estimated 9,000 government army. Between 2,000 to 3,000 Jacobites retreated to Ruthven Barracks, where they regathered and awaited further orders, yet when word came, it was that Prince Charles was making his escape back to France, and that they should flee and save themselves.

The Culloden Battle Memorial Cairn

needless to say, the battleground is said to be haunted, with the sounds of battle cries and swords clashing on the anniversary of the battle. Birds are also said not to be heard on the battlefield, and anyone visiting will note how eerily quiet it can seem at times. Full bodied apparitions are also said to be seen, including highlanders standing close to their clan graves, and soldiers lying slain on the battlefield.

<u>Ruthven Barracks</u>

Ruthven Barracks were built between 1719 and 1721 to house Government Troops to try to suppress the Jacobite Uprisings.

The Ruins of Ruthven Barracks

Prior to the barracks being built, this was the site of Ruthven Castle which, like many castles in Scotland, carry a tale of devastation being caused by the Devil. Although the construction date is uncertain, the castle is documented from 1229, when it was the home of William Comyn, the Lord of Badenoch. However, it was not until1371, when King Robert II gave the castle and lands to his son, Alexander Stewart, that the castle gained its dark reputation.

Alexander Stewart was, by all accounts, very much his own man and not one to be hesitant in expressing his views, or using his power. With castles across the highlands, he was responsible for imposing the authority of the crown throughout the region, something he did with brutal effectiveness, earning him the nickname 'The Wolf of Badenoch.' To just cause him offence was enough to be imprisoned, or worse. His methods were disapproved of by the King's Council, who formally expressed their concern in 1388, but it was not until 1389 that it became clear just how far he was prepared to go.

Having failed to have children with his wife, Alexander Stewart sought the aid of the Bishop of Moray to end his marriage on the basis she was unable to bear children. The Bishop however supported his wife, and refused his request. Unconcerned, Alexander Stewart had her removed and moved his mistress in, resulting in him being excommunicated by the Bishop of Moray.

The unfortunate monk who arrived to deliver the news was imprisoned in the Pit Prison and in 1390, Alexander Stewart marched his army to Elgin, base of the Bishop of Moray, where he burned the Cathedral to the ground, and destroyed much of the town. He also destroyed a large part of nearby Pluscarden Abbey.

It is believed this action led to an encounter, widely said to have occurred in 1390, when a tall stranger arrived at Ruthven Castle late one night and requested to meet Alexander Stewart, before challenging him to a game of cards (some accounts suggest it was a game of chess). The game continued through the night, with a mighty storm arising just after midnight. Whether this signified the stranger winning, or the game passing into the Sunday, varies between the re-telling of the story.

Those attending the castle the following morning reported finding all of the staff lying on the ground around the castle, dead and charred as though struck by lightning. Only Alexander Stewart remained inside, also dead though his body was unmarked, other than the tacks holding the soles of his shoes in place had been ripped out. Gossip spread that the stranger had been the Devil himself, collecting Alexander's soul.

Alexander Stewart did however die in 1405, with his body laid to rest at Dunkeld Cathedral, and so if there is any truth in the story, it must have happened later than most accounts say. Although the castle is long gone, the well within the ruins of Ruthven Barracks is said to be the original well that served Ruthven Castle, and it is around this that visitors report unexplained activity including cold spots, feelings of being watched, nausea and a general sensation of unease.

Findlater Castle, Aberdeenshire

As far as castles go, the location of Findlater is impressive, perched not just on, but in, a rocky outcrop accessible only by a long, narrow path with sheer drops on either side. Drawbridges once made crossing this uneven path easier, but these have long gone.

The remains of Findlater Castle

A castle has stood on the site since Viking times, with the name Findlater coming from the Norse words 'Fyn' meaning white, and 'Leiter' meaning cliff, which relates to the local quartz rock which can give exposed cliffs a white appearance. The earliest record of the castle is from the 1246, with it being fortified in the 1260's by King Alexander III in preparation for an expected attack along the Moray coast by King Hakon IV of Norway. Although it is believed the Norsemen took and occupied the castle before their ultimate defeat at the Battle of Largs, no records are held relating to the castle from this time.

The structure that remains today was built in the 14th century for Sir John Sinclair, although this belief is based on the design of the castle being similar to Rosslyn Castle, the seat of the Sinclair family. The first documented records are from 1455 when King James II granted permission to Sir Walter Ogilvy for the castle to be extended and the defences strengthened. As mentioned earlier, access to the castle is via a clifftop pathway, with 2 deep natural trenches where drawbridges once aided the crossing, and with the castle sitting approximately 50 feet above the surrounding shoreline, it is difficult to imagine the work that went into any construction.

While the castle may have initially been designed to protect against overseas invaders, it was the internal battles for power in Scotland that would bring the most notable attack to its walls. The Ogilvy family clashed over loyalties to Mary, Queen of Scots, with Sir Alexander Ogilvy finally disinheriting his son, James, and passing the castle to Sir John Gordon, the son of the Earl of Huntly.

James Ogilvy, however, held considerable influence with the monarchy, and knowing the Gordon family were rebelling against Queen Mary's authority, he convinced her to visit the castle. She was refused entry, and in response ordered her army to besiege the castle. Although the castle defences held, the Gordon family were eventually defeated at the Battle of Corrichie, and John Gordon was charged with treason, and be-headed, following which the castle was returned to the Ogilvy family.

The fate of the castle was however sealed, and in the 1600's the Ogilvie family moved to nearby Cullen House, which provided far more comfortable accommodation and the castle was abandoned. Although there are several reported hauntings connected to the castle, it is from this sudden departure and the building being left to decay that the ghost story most commonly told by locals originates.

It is said that a nanny was caring for one of the infant sons of the Ogilvy family, and as she comforted him to sleep in her arms she took him to the window to get some sea air. The child, however, acted excitedly to the open air, and wriggled in the nanny's arms, causing her to lose her grip and he fell to the sea below. The nanny desperately tried to grab him, but in doing so lost her balance and fell from the window herself. Her ghostly figure is reported to still be seen to this day, wandering the ruins looking for the child she lost.

A visit to the castle is well worth it, but it is not easy to find! A sign from the main road points you in the rough direction, but you then need to make your way along single track roads, to an unmarked carpark and then walk around half a mile along the side of a field (make sure to check out the doocot on the way). But the view when you get there is amazing!

St Bridget's Church, Fife

On the banks of the River Forth, close to the town of Dalgety Bay, sits St Bridget's Kirk. Built in the 12th century, the kirk was once at the centre of a small community in the village of Dalgety. This was a thriving area, however, the growth of the mining industry resulted in the inhabitants leaving to seek new employment, taking up residence in the miner's cottages that were built close to the mines.

St Bridget's Church

By 1830, the village was mostly deserted and the kirk ceased to be used, which would have resulted in anyone remaining to also leave. Today there are no visible signs of the village, yet the kirk remains as a roofless ruin, with only some original features remaining.

While visiting the atmospheric kirk and kirkyard, and taking in the quiet and peaceful area, it is easy to imagine that the ancient building could be haunted. However, the ghosts on this site are not of the type normally associated with a church, instead it is phantom pirates that are seen and heard in the area.

So why do these phantoms roam the area? The port of Leith, which sits to the south east on the opposite banks of the River Forth, was a major port for imports and exports which attracted pirates. It is known that in the 14th and 15th century there was French and possibly English pirates operating in the Forth, attacking the ships and religious establishments on the islands that sit in the bay.

Overlooking the Graveyard and the River Forth

It is believed that after one of the ships was sunk, some of those onboard drowned and were washed ashore on the beach in front of the Kirk. The bodies were buried in the surrounding woodland out with the church boundary, and so not in consecrated ground, leaving their spirits unable to rest in peace and to forever wander the area. It is reported that the pirates are most commonly witnessed in autumn, and it is more common to hear them as they walk around the church, often accompanied by a sensation of being watched, rather than seeing the figures.

The Tale of Johnny One Arm

The city of Edinburgh has numerous tales of hauntings, some of which are folklore, while others are backed by historical records. The tale of Johnny One Arm is perhaps best described as a mixture of both.

Dalry House, Edinburgh

The story surrounds a man named John Chiesley, who lived in the Dalry area of the city in the 17th century. By all accounts, he was an argumentative and violent character, who did not shy away from making threats against people he felt had done him wrong, no matter what their status in society. He was married to Margaret Nicholson, and despite the marriage being described as a miserable one, at least for Margaret, they had ten children together. Eventually Margaret decided that she could not stay in the relationship any longer, and they separated.

Chiesley had a sizeable estate, and a legal dispute followed the separation, which was heard by the Lord President, Sir George Lockhart, a well-respected solicitor in the city. It would seem Chiesley was confident things would go in his favour, as women at that time had few rights. However, it was not unknown for Sir George to go against what the community or the legal profession may expect and to make a decision based on the facts.

After hearing the case, he ruled not only that the separation was legal, but ordered Chiesley to pay Margaret the sum of 1,700 Merks annually, which would equate to around £93, a large sum at that time. Chiesley was furious, and vowed that Sir George would pay with his life. A threat that he would repeat several times in the following months.

Despite being warned of the risk, Sir George paid little attention and continued to go about his life and business as normal. On Easter Sunday, 1689, he had attended a church service at the city's St. Giles Cathedral, as he usually did, after which he walked back to his home, accompanied by his cousins, Lord Castlehill and Daniel Lockhart. Unknown to them, John Chiesley had been waiting outside the cathedral and had followed them. As they approached the house, Chiesley pulled out a pistol and shot Sir George in the back.

Lady Lockhart, Sir George's wife, was unwell at the time and was being treated by the town's Dr Hay inside the house. Both heard the gunshot and rushed outside to see what had happened. Dr Hay tried to help Sir George, but found that the bullet had passed straight through his chest, killing him almost immediately. In the meantime, others who had witnessed the incident grabbed Chiesley, who put up little resistance, instead declaring that he had taught the President how to do justice.

Given that the crime was carried out in such a public manner, authorisation was granted to torture Chiesley to determine whether he had any accomplices who had aided him in the murder, yet he maintained he had acted alone. He stated that he had carried his pistol in his jacket on other occasions previously, waiting for the right moment to carry out the killing. He gave his reasons as his belief that Sir George had made an unjust ruling against him, yet refused to confirm whether that was the ruling in favour of his ex-wife.

With so many witnesses and an open confession, Chiesley was sentenced to death. On 3rd April, 1689, he was taken from Edinburgh Tollbooth to the Mercat Cross, where his right hand, that being the one in which he held the pistol, was cut off before he was hung. His body was then moved to be suspended by chains, with the pistol hanging around his neck, and his severed hand was nailed to the West Port, both as a warning to all. A few days later however, the body went missing.

It was speculated that the body had been retrieved by his family and taken to be hidden at his mansion, Dalry House. As rumours circulated, the maids at the house started to refuse to enter the kitchen at the back of the house after dark, as this was where it was thought the body had been hidden. Family tales started to circulate that a huge phantom figure was seen on occasion, floating from the back of the house to a recess in the garden wall before vanishing.

People also started to claim that they had seen the ghost of a man running around the area, as well as at the

Royal Mile, screaming insanely and waving his arm with a bloody stump where the hand had been removed. As the story of the phantom grew, parents started to use it to scare their children into behaving or the ghost of Johnny One Arm would get them.

The story does not; however, end there. It is claimed that long after the tale of the hauntings had become local folklore, a stone seat in the recess of the garden wall where the phantom had been seen by the maids had to be removed. Within the structure, a skeleton was found, complete with the exception of the right hand, which was missing. An alternative version states the bones were found beneath a hearth in a cottage on the former estate. Again, it was said that the right hand was missing, but also that there was a pistol mixed in amongst the remains.

The body was said to have been given a proper burial at an undisclosed location, after which the hauntings ceased. A few months later; however, people started to claim they felt an unseen hand try to grab them as they walked down Advocates Close in the city. A connection was made with Johnny One Arm, although the reason is not clear.

Perhaps with its close vicinity to St. Giles it was where John Chiesley hid, waiting for Sir George while gripping the pistol tightly. It is suggested that after the rest of his body had been buried, Chiesley's missing hand was reaching out to try to join it.

Pistols at Dawn

Just outside Kirkcaldy in Fife, sits Balmuto Castle, a stronghold dating back to the 15th century, which has now been fully restored to a private home.

Balmuto Castle

The castle was originally built for Sir John Boswell, with it being extensively remodelled and extended by successive generations. At the end of the 18th century, following the death of his father, the castle was inherited by 19 year old Sir Alexander Boswell, who soon after ended his studies in law to concentrate on improving agriculture on the castle estate. He was also a poet and, leaving the castle in the hands of a relative, went on to hold a commanding officer role in the cavalry, and pursue a career in politics.

Boswell was a member of the Tory Party who were, at that time, arch opponents of the Whigs, the predecessors of today's Liberal Democrats. By 1820, he was; however becoming increasingly disillusioned with politics, feeling he was not receiving the respect he deserved. With the profits from his estate dropping due to some poor decisions and increasing costs, he resigned from politics in early 1821 and returned to his Edinburgh home.

Although he was no longer a Member of Parliament, it seems his disliking for the Whigs remained strong and, in 1822, he sent a number of articles anonymously to the Glasgow Sentinel Newspaper, which in turn published them. The articles were particularly scathing regarding James Stuart of Dunearn, a writer and Whig politician, who in turn sued the paper for libel. In the following legal proceedings, the original manuscripts were made available to James Stuart, who knew Boswell personally and recognised his handwriting.

When confronted, Boswell refused to either admit nor deny he had written the articles, and stated James Stuart had all the information that he needed. Unsatisfied with the response, Stuart took the rather unusual step to challenge Boswell to a duel.

It should be noted that duels of that time did not occur in the manner most believe today. They were organised events, with rules setting out the process. Each party had to appoint an assistant known as a 'second,' whose role it was to oversee the proceedings. The challenger could decide whether they would take turns to fire, or whether they would fire at the same time.

Since duelling pistols were notoriously inaccurate, if neither had been hit the challenger could decide whether they were satisfied their grievance had been settled, or whether they wanted to fire again. Although it was deemed against the rules, this gave the option for both parties to agree to deliberately miss, and neither to lose their honour.

After a failed attempt to hold the duel in Edinburgh, the date was set for it to take place on 26th March, 1822, at Auchtertool, a few miles from Kirkcaldy. The distance between the men was agreed at 12 paces, with identical pistols being loaded with the same amount of gunpowder by the seconds. Stuart had decided they would both fire at the same time, and as they faced each other, Boswell raised his pistol into the air before both took aim and, on the command, fired.

Boswell missed, but Stuart's shot hit his opponent in the shoulder, breaking his collarbone before travelling down to his spine. A door from Balmuto Castle, which was just a short distance away, was used as a makeshift stretcher, and he was taken to the castle for treatment. Unfortunately, despite the best efforts of 2 local surgeons, Sir Alexander Boswell died on 27th March.

James Stuart found himself facing a murder charge, although he was subsequently found not guilty. Few could believe that a man who had never held a gun before could kill a seasoned military commander in a duel, but in the papers from the trial it was revealed that Boswell had written that he held no ill will against Stuart, and intended to deliberately miss.

The action of raising his pistol into the air before any shots were fired was likely to be intended to indicate this to Stuart, however, as he had no knowledge of such things, he had not realised the significance of this action. Stuart stated that had he been aware of Boswell's feelings and intentions, he would not have proceeded with the duel.

Since his death, the ghost of Alexander Boswell has been seen in the library area of Balmuto Castle, with it being commonly told that it was the library door which was used as a stretcher. The castle was abandoned in 1896, and was sold as a ruin in 1951 when the last of the direct family died with no heirs. It was; however, bought in 1960 by an American descendent of the family, who restored it to its former glory. Sir Alexander is believed to still be seen within the castle, with his spirit being affectionately referred to as 'Sandy.'

The Cursed Laird of Buckholm Tower

On a remote hillside overlooking the town of Galashiels in the Scottish Borders, stands the ruins of Buckholm Tower.

Buckholm Tower-house

The property was originally built as a defensive tower house in the 16th century for the Pringle family, who had been awarded the lands in 1524 by the King of Scotland. Standing at just three storeys it was not a large property as far as tower houses go, although the family did have other property in the area.

The tower house was a standard L-shape, with the ground floor being a vaulted chamber with no access to the upper floors and the main entrance being at first floor level, as was common at the time. A small, separate tower was attached to the side houses and the stairs and a two storey extension was added during the 18th century, by which time the risks of attack were dwindling and families sought to make property more suited for comfortable living. It is not clear exactly when the property was abandoned, but it is believed it was occupied up until the 1930s.

During the 17th century the tower gained a dark and ominous reputation, due to the laird of the time, James Pringle. James was said to be a particularly unpleasant and cruel man, to the extent that his wife left him, taking their child with her, an act almost unheard of at that time in history. This is reported to have only driven Pringle to become more bitter, and he took out his temper and vengeance on the Covenanters, a religious faction who opposed the religious settlement imposed on Scotland following the Union of the Crowns in 1603.

Pringle was a Royalist and so, as enemies to the crown, he too would have considered the Covenanters to be his enemy. Aided by two large hounds, he gained quite a reputation in his ability to hunt their soldiers and so when approached by a troop of Royal Dragoons to assist in locating a local group of Covenanters, he was only too happy to assist.

With his in-depth knowledge of the area, he suspected he knew where they would be hiding, and led the Dragoons to the location. He was correct; however, the Covenanters had either been notified of their approach, or had seen them, and had already made their escape, apart from two. They found a man who was known to Pringle, named George Elliott, and his son, William. George had been flung from his horse and William had chosen to stay with his injured father to try to help him.

Already frustrated that most of the Covenanters had escaped, Pringle became even more annoyed when the Captain of the Dragoons instructed him to take the prisoners back to Buckholm Tower and hold them there until the next day, when they would be taken to face trial. Pringle wanted to slay them there and then. He did; however, do as he was instructed, and locked the captives in the ground floor chamber, before retiring to his private quarters where he is said to have started drinking heavily, becoming increasingly enraged at having to hold the men.

Eventually, his temper got the better of him, and he stormed to the ground floor chamber. The servants reputedly heard heavy blows being delivered to, they assumed, one of the Covenanters, as they also could hear a man crying out in agony. After some time, everything went quiet. According to the story told, as Pringle was leaving the chamber, he saw a woman approaching. As she got closer, he recognised her as George Elliot's wife. She had learned of her husband and son's capture, and had come to the tower out of fear due to the Laird's reputation.

Confronted with Pringle covered in blood, she demanded to know where her loved ones were. Pringle was only too happy to show her and dragged her to where they had been held. She was horrified to find that he had assaulted not just one of the men, as the servants had believed, but he had beaten them both to death. Their bodies were hung from a beam, some say by meat hooks. Heart-broken, she sobbed a curse at the Laird, before fleeing.

The exact words of the curse are not documented, however, ever since the Laird believed he was being pursued by hounds, just as he had pursued his victims. During his sleep his servants would often rush to his aid after hearing him shouting from his bed chamber, only to find him thrashing about as though fighting off an invisible assailant. Even on his deathbed, he was said to have appeared as though he was fighting off an attacker.

As the first anniversary of his death approached, the servants were stunned to witness the Laird running towards the tower, along with the sounds of howling hounds, as though in pursuit. Loud bangs followed at the door and the Laird shouting to be let in, before everything fell silent. When checking, the servants found no one there. This continued to happen for a few days, before stopping on the anniversary of his death. In the following years, the events are said to have been repeated annually, on or around the anniversary.

The cries of poor George and William Elliot are also said to still be heard echoing from the chamber in which they were so cruelly beaten to death, and rumours of blood stains on the beam from which they were hung persist, with the claim that they cannot be cleaned off.

The Murdered Blacksmith of Kildrummy Castle

In the remote countryside of Aberdeenshire, the magnificent ruins of Kildrummy Castle can be found, along with an eerie atmosphere encountered by visitors.

The entrance to Kildrummy Castle

This stronghold dates back to around 1250, when it was built for the Earl of Mar. King Edward I of England visited twice, the second time accompanied by his most trusted stonemason, Master James of St. George. Similarities have been noted between the gatehouse of Harlech Castle in Wales, which was designed by Master James, and the gatehouse at Kildrummy, leading it to be widely believed that King Edward and his mason were influential in the design.

This is probably something King Edward regretted. The Earls of Mar were supporters of the Bruce family, and when the newly crowned Robert the Bruce launched his military campaign against the English King in 1306, he had his wife and daughter sent to Kildrummy Castle for their own safety. King Robert's brother, Neil Bruce, successfully held off successive attacks of the castle, led by Prince Edward, son of Edward I.

It seems the increased protection added by his father ended up working against them. Eventually the castle did fall, when a fire broke out in the great hall, killing some of those inside and forcing Neil Bruce to surrender. He was taken to be executed while King Robert's wife and daughter were taken and held at the Tower of London.

The English forces caused considerable damage to the castle in an attempt to stop it being used again, but it was taken back by the Scots and repaired. It would go on to change hands and be fought over several times, an indication of its importance.

In 1335, the Earl of Atholl, David III Strathbogie, who was a supporter of the exiled King Balliol, attacked the castle. Inside was an army of Bruce Loyalists, led by Dame Christian Bruce, who successfully held it until her husband, Sir Andrew Murray, returned and defeated the Earl's forces at the Battle of Culbean.

It was later taken by the Royalist forces of King David II, before ownership passed to Alexander Stewart, the Wolf of Badenoch, through his marriage to Isabella, the Countess of Marr. Upon his death in the mid-1340s, King James I took possession of the castle rather than allow it to pass to the rightful heir, and it was extended and strengthened.

In 1507 the estate was gifted to the Elphinstone family who occupied the castle until 1654, when it was attacked and taken by supporters of Oliver Cromwell. In 1689 it was taken by the Jacobite forces, who were defeated by the army of Graham of Claverhouse, Viscount of Dundee, in 1690, who in turn had the castle destroyed. Ownership returned to John Erskine, the Earl of Mar who carried out restoration and was a principal figure in the 1715 Jacobite uprising.

In 1716, Erskine travelled to France with James Stuart and lived the rest of his life in exile there. Keen to ensure it was never again used by their opponents, the government forces had the castle dismantled and the stones were used as a quarry for the construction of many of the surrounding buildings.

With such a long and turbulent history, it would be fair to say there have been many incidents which could result in the castle being haunted. It is; however, believed to be from the fire in 1306 that the haunting originated. Had it not been for the fire, it is likely Sir Neil Bruce would have successfully held off King Edward, changing the course of history. The fire was, however, no accident, it was caused deliberately by a blacksmith named Osborne.

It is not known whether the English forces sought some inside help, or whether he approached the English to strike a deal, but it is documented that having reached an agreement, Osborne dropped a red-hot metal rod through an opening into the Great Hall, which was being used as the grain store at the time. With the fire raging and the castle enclosure filling with smoke, Bruce had no option but to surrender, giving the victory to King Edward.

Things did not; however, end as Osborne the Blacksmith may have envisaged. It is said the deal was that in return for setting the fire, he would be given as much gold as he could carry. But it seems no one likes a traitor. According to the legend, to judge how much gold Osborne should receive, he was pinned to the ground and molten gold was poured into his mouth! With such a horrific ending, it is said his spirit energy continues to roam the castle, perhaps forever repenting his actions.

The Phantom Prior of Blackfriars Chapel

A curious ruin sits on South Street in the town of St Andrews, which most locals walk past without as much as a glance, while visitors take photographs without much knowledge of the building's past. A few; however, will catch a glimpse of a mysterious hooded figure wandering the grounds behind it, sometime said to be almost blinking in and out of view.

The remains of Blackfriars Chapel

The ruin is in fact the remains of a Dominican friary, known as Blackfriars Chapel, a Scheduled Monument, noted as one of only three surviving Dominican Chapels with standing remains that exists in Scotland. The history of the chapel is short, and relatively uneventful. The Dominican Friars were known as the Blackfriars due to the colour of the cloak they wore, and when the Friary was completed around 1525, it was home to five. Although there are no surviving plans, it is believed the Friary occupied most of the lawns which sit behind the chapel, which are now the grounds of Madras College.

The Friars would have lived a relatively peaceful life in St Andrews, until 1559 when the full force of the Protestant Reformation arrived. The Reformation had swept through Europe, with Catholic countries converting to the Protestant faith. St. Andrews Cathedral was the home of the Catholic church in Scotland, making the town a prime target for the reformers. Blackfriars was one of the first buildings to be attacked, with it being recorded that the monks were violently banished and the building extensively damaged.

The reported haunting does not; however, relate to the demise of the friary, but to an incident that happened much earlier, and a critical point in the early stages of the reformation. A young student named Patrick Hamilton, having travelled across Europe, returned to St Andrews to take up his studies at the university. When travelling, he had heard influential reformers, such as Martin Luther, deliver sermons, and Patrick was keen to share his knowledge. Needless to say, that was not a wise move at a university with direct links to the Catholic church and in the home-town of the Archbishop of St Andrews.

Patrick was allowed to go about his day to day activities with little interference for several months, although he would have been aware of the risks he was taking as he fled back to mainland Europe for a short while. He was eventually arrested and after a mock trial was found guilty of heresy. On 29th February 1528, he was chained to a stake above a small pile of wood in front of St Salvator's Chapel, having been sentenced to be burned alive. What followed was horrific. Due to a number of errors made in the hurried attempt to make an example of him, it took Hamilton 6 hours to finally succumb to the flames.

One of those who played a key role in the build up to Patrick Hamilton's death, was Alexander Campbell, a Dominican prior from Blackfriars Friary. He won Hamilton's trust by acting as though he was interested in what he had to say, while all the time he was gathering evidence to be used against him. At his execution, the Blackfriars urged Hamilton to renounce the Protestant faith, and when he refused it was said that Campbell publicly condemned him to face the judgement of Christ.

There are two versions of what happened afterwards to Alexander Campbell. Some writings tell that he suffered burns during the execution when a pocket of gunpowder exploded, and that his injuries became infected, while others say he was struck down with an unidentified illness shortly after. All attempts to treat him failed, and he died soon afterwards. It was felt by many that it was him rather than Patrick Hamilton who had been judged by Christ, and that his phantom still wanders the grounds of the Friary looking for forgiveness.

The Druid of Kirkmichael

The village of Kirkmichael, close to Pitlochry in Perthshire, is not dissimilar to many rural villages in Scotland. It gives a picturesque mix of old cottages and more modern buildings, and with a river passing through its centre, it offers the traveller a place to stop and enjoy the scenery.

Kirkmichael Church

As you enter the village from Blairgowrie, you pass the church, which sits above the river, and the old Manse on the higher ground to the right. Again, there is nothing that would leap out at you, as far as churches go there is nothing out of the ordinary, and the manse cannot be seen from the roadside. Both are ancient buildings, the Manse was predominately constructed in its current form in 1760, although it incorporates part of a much earlier building, which dated back to 1380. Even this was a more modern building than the original, as it is stated a dwelling has stood on the site for over 1,200 years. It is in this area around the church and manse where a terrifying phantom is reported to walk and blood curdling screams are said to be heard.

Despite the peaceful and relaxing feel the village has today, Kirkmichael has seen more than its fair share of violent history. There were battles in the surrounding hills during the first century between the Romans and the Celts, and in 1653 it was reported that Oliver Cromwell himself stayed in the manse during his invasion of Scotland while his New Model Army did battle in the Church grounds.

Kirkmichael is not far from Killiekrankie and it is quite likely that the defeated Government troops fled to, and were pursued through, the village after the Jacobite victory at the Battle of Killiekrankie in 1689. In 1715 the Jacobite forces again gathered in the town to prepare for their march south, yet it is none of these events that lead to the reported haunting.

A spring carrying water that is believed to have healing properties runs beneath the Manse and emerges at the roadside opposite the church, and this may give a clue to the land's past, as would the description given of the ghost, said to be a robed figure with a long beard and carrying a golden sickle. The whole area was in fact once the sacred lands of a Druid temple.

In writings dated from 1807, it was recorded that a vast body of Druid remains still existed, which comprised of a huge cairn measuring over 8m tall and more than 80m around. A large number of smaller cairns were positioned in groups of 8 or 10 around this larger one, along with several stones, some still standing, some fallen.

A rocking stone also could be found within the parish. These were massive stones perched on top of smaller stones allowing them to be rocked by hand. They were often used for judgement of those accused of wrongdoing, with them being set in motion and the position in which they finally came to rest symbolising whether the accused was innocent or guilty.

As for the site of the manse itself, in 1899 it was recorded that, although nothing has remained for a very long time and historical maps no longer show it, two thousand years ago a stone circle had stood on the site, and it was the fact this was already considered to be holy ground to the natives that it was chosen for the construction of the first church. This rather pleasant-sounding description is likely to be different from the reality, with the ancient places of worship destroyed to make way for the new religion.

It is believed that the figure seen roaming the lands is the spirit of a Druid Priest, still protecting his temple, possibly energised by the flowing healing water that passes below the ground. Although reports suggest that he is residual and does not interact, his image strikes fear to those who see him. Yet it is the screams that cause most distress to those unfortunate to hear them.

The origin of these cries may also be connected to the flowing water in the area, and the Priest's Well. This was formerly known as the Heathen Well, with heathen in biblical terms meaning one who does not acknowledge the God of the Bible, which would include Pagans. Such was the size of the temple, it is believed sacrifices to the gods would have been offered here, and the cries are those of the humans who were slain in the sacrificial ceremonies.

The Church of Skulls

In the year 1004, during the Viking invasions of the North of Scotland, a great sea storm forced a fleet of Viking ships to seek shelter from storms just off the Banff coast in the Moray Firth. With the storms continuing, making it too dangerous to leave the protection of the bay, supplies on the ships began to dwindle, and became insufficient to eventually make the journey home once the storms had passed.

Looking over the ruins of St John's to Gardenstown

A party of around 600 Vikings were sent ashore to pillage the local area close to where the village of Gardenstown now sits. With no signs of any habitation, it had been hoped this would be a swift mission to seize any supplies they could before setting sail again.

However, unknown to them one of the local rulers, the Thane of Buchan, had been watching since their ships first anchored. Knowing that an attack was likely, he had gathered a large army as a precaution. When the Vikings landed, the Thane's army attacked from their hiding places, and a bloody battle was fought, with even the local women making makeshift maces by removing their stockings and filling them with stones from the beach.

The Vikings were caught off guard by the surprise attack, and were soon overwhelmed. With the route back to their boats on the beach cut off, a small group of survivors fled across a river and up a steep hill where they found a position surrounded by cliffs making it easier to defend. With unobstructed views, they could see any advancing local forces, and holding the higher ground they were able to beat back any attempted attacks.

Knowing they would be visible to those on the Viking boats still in the bay, and that it would be a just a matter of time before a rescue party was sent, the Thane of Buchan sought divine intervention and prayed to St. John. In return for help to defeat the Viking invaders, he promised to build a church in his name.

Shortly after, a change in weather conditions created cover for the Scots to advance on the Viking camp unseen. In the surprise attack that followed, the last of the Norsemen were slaughtered in a battle so violent that two natural hollows in the ground above the church became known as the Pits of Blood, due to the number of Viking bodies thrown there.

True to his word, the Thane had a church built, dedicated to St. John, on the very site of the Viking camp. Locally, the church was known as 'the Church of Skulls,' due to the heads of the 3 Viking leaders being placed on view in purpose-built alcoves in the church walls.

The original church was rebuilt around 1513, and it was abandoned around 1830 when a new parish church was built. Two of the Viking skulls were stolen, with the third being reported to be held at Banff Museum, although it is not clear whether it remains there. It is said that, on occasion, the cries of the fallen Viking soldiers can still be heard across the valley, and visitors to the church report glimpsing figures that disappear when they turn for a better look. Perhaps these are the spirits of the Viking leaders, still looking for their missing heads.

The Haunting of Hermitage Castle

With its massive curtain walls with virtually no openings, Hermitage Castle is both an impressive and an intimidating sight.

The formidable ruins of Hermiston Castle

The castle lies close to the border between Scotland and England, an area that was heavily fought over for centuries resulting in the heavy fortifications being an important part of the initial construction. It changed hands numerous times during the battles for the disputed lands, and it was not until the Union of the Crowns in 1603 that the risk of attack started to decline.

The present castle was constructed in the 14th century, but a castle previously stood on the site built for Lord De Soules in the mid-13th century. It is Lord De Soules who is central in a gruesome myth surrounding the castle.

Referred to as 'Bad Lord De Soulis' in the folklore, he was described as being a giant of a man with immense physical strength who was involved in black magic, having been taught by a local warlock. In order to use his magic, it is said he kidnapped, imprisoned, and murdered local children.

According to the legend, Bad Lord De Soulis was protected by Redcap, a form of particularly malicious Faerie or Goblin, and his Redcap had cast a spell which made it impossible for De Soulis to be harmed by steel or rope, making it virtually impossible for the locals to restrain or kill him.

Eventually, however, they did finally fight back against De Soulis and, having overpowered him they wrapped him in a sheet of lead to bind and restrain him. They then carried him to a large cauldron at a stone circle at and area named Ninestane Rig, and they threw him in. The raging fire below eventually caused the lead to melt, and De Soulis was boiled in the molten metal. The fate of the Bad Lord was part of a ballad written by Dr John Leyden (1775 – 1811);

'On a circle of stone they placed the pot,
On a circle of stones but barely nine,
They heated it up red and fiery hot,
Till the burnished brass did glimmer and shine.

They rolled him up in a sheet of lead,
A sheet of lead for a funeral pall,
They plunged him in the cauldron red,
and melted him, lead, bones and all.'

De Soulis is said to still haunt the area around the castle

with a large figure being seen on occasion both in the castle grounds and inside the castle. Workmen carrying out restoration work to the castle witnessed the figure looking out from a window on an inaccessible upper floor, which may cast doubt on whether this is in fact De Soulis, as the current castle did not exist during his lifetime.

Of course if it is not him, it raises of the question of who it is that haunts the ruins. Perhaps it is James Hepburn, 4th Earl of Bothwell, who was taken to the castle after being injured in a fight with cattle thieves in October 1566. It is said his secret lover, Mary, Queen of Scots, made the dangerous journey to be with him, following which she herself fell seriously ill and nearly passed away at her house in Jedburgh.

There are reports of children's cries being heard within the walls of the castle, which are believed to be the spirits of those imprisoned by De Soulis still tied to the land. Disembodied screams of agony are also said to echo from the direction of Ninestane Rig, which are believed to be the evil lord reliving the agonies of his final moments.

Cathedral House Hotel, Glasgow

The Cathedral House Hotel stands close to Glasgow Cathedral and the infamous Glasgow Necropolis, a vast Victorian Cemetery where many of the elite of the day are laid to rest in impressive tombs.

Cathedral House Hotel

Built in 1896, the hotel was originally constructed to provide temporary accommodation for prisoners being released from the nearby Duke Street Prison. The prison, originally known as Bridewell, opened in 1798 and housed both male and female prisoners. In 1825, following the 1823 Gaol Act, a new prison was built on the site, which is when it became known as Duke Street Prison.

The conditions inside were terrible with severe overcrowding and, following further prison reforms, Barlinnie Prison was built in 1882 with the intention to replace Duke Street, but numbers remained so high Duke Street remained open, predominantly as a women's prison, until 1955.

Long-term prisoners were given accommodation in the property that would later become the Cathedral House Hotel, with the intention that it would give them the opportunity to adapt to normal day to day life, re-establishing themselves into the community while looking for employment. Following the closure of the jail, the building was used as a Sunday School and to provide accommodation for staff working at the Cathedral before it was converted into a hotel. With the horrors the former convicts had experienced within the jail, it seems that some either left an emotional imprint on the building, or returned there after death, perhaps due to it being a place they felt genuinely safe.

Reports of paranormal activity include guests feeling someone push past them on the stairs, yet when they check there is nobody there. Ghostly children are also witnessed, and it is not known whether these are in fact young ladies who may have been held in the jail, or children who were reunited with their mothers upon their release.

Certainly some of the experiences indicate young children, with reports of hearing the footsteps of them running around on the top floor, accompanied by the sound of them giggling, as though they are playing. Other reported activity includes the furniture being found to have been notably moved in empty areas and rooms, along with unexplained electrical faults.

It is not; however, only the hotel that has reports of unexplained happenings. Following the demolition of the prison, a housing estate was built on the site, and there are claims of encounters there too. These are mostly thought to be connected to the hangings that took place within the prison. From 1865, executions were made private and twelve people were hung within the walls of the prison, all having been found guilty of murder.

This included the last woman to be hung in Scotland, Susan Newell, in 1923, following her conviction on the charge of strangling a 13 year old paperboy to death. Those hung within the prison were also buried there, and although there is some debate on where the bodies lie, when the housing estate was built one area of land was left untouched other than being landscaped, and the rumour started that the developers refused to build there due to it being the burial ground.

Sightings of a phantom woman walking through the area have been made, and while some speculate she may be one of the former prisoners, there are also claims that the sound of keys rattling accompany these sightings, leading to the belief she may in fact have been a guard, still carrying out her duties as she did in life. A spectral dog is also reported to roam the area, believed to be a replay of prison life.

A darker entity is reported to lurk within one of the houses built on the site. Residents have reported hearing footsteps behind them and when turning to see who it is, they saw the shadow form of a figure rushing towards them with its arms raised, before vanishing in front of them. It is said that the figure is missing a hand, perhaps a sign of an injury sustained while imprisoned and a reason for the seemingly angry spirit to remain. The phantom dog has also been seen within the property, mostly around children, leading to the belief that the dog protects the youngsters from the shadow figure.

The Grey Lady of Sweetheart Abbey, Dumfries and Galloway

In the year 1223, Lord John Balliol, Lord of Gainford and of Barnard Castle which sits in County Durham, England, married Lady Dervogilla of Dumfries, Scotland, bringing two of the most influential families from both nations together.

Sweetheart Abbey

Lord Balliol held several prominent roles, including the protection of the young King of Scotland, Alexander III and as an advisor to King Henry III of England. In 1263, together with Lady Dervogilla, in order to settle a land dispute with the Bishop of Durham, they founded the Balliol College in Oxford to provide education to the poor.

On 25th of October 1268, Lord Balliol died leaving the vast wealth of their combined estates to his heartbroken wife. To safeguard the work they had carried out, she immediately secured the future of their college by making a permanent endowment, and it remains in use as part of the University of Oxford to this day, laying claim to three former British Prime Ministers within its alumni.

On 10th April 1273, she signed a charter to establish an abbey, known simply as New Abbey, in memory of her late husband, and the substantial building with a central bell tower was constructed from local red sandstone close to the town of Dumfries in Scotland. The Abbey was not the only act of devotion Lady Dervogilla made to her husband. After his death, she had felt unable to live parted from him, and so had his heart embalmed and placed in an ivory casket that she carried with her at all times, and she intended to ensure this continued after her own death.

She left instructions that when she passed away she was to be buried in the Abbey, with the casket with her husband's heart buried beside her. When she died on 28th January 1290, her wishes were carried out, leading to the Abbey becoming affectionately known as Sweetheart Abbey, a name which stuck.

Their son, John Balliol, would go on to successful contest the Crown, becoming King of Scotland in November 1292. The rightful heir had been fiercely disputed, and King Edward I of England had been asked to assist. King Edward, seeing an opportunity, had insisted that all those who staked a claim did so with the agreement that whoever became King would rule Scotland under the sovereignty of the English Monarch.

As a result Balliol was a weak ruler, controlled by King Edward. In 1294, he decided enough was enough and refused Edward's request that Scottish soldiers be sent to assist in his war against France. In an ultimate act of defiance, Balliol instead signed an agreement with Philip IV of France against England. King Edward's response was to invade Scotland, capture and humiliate King Balliol and take the Stone of Destiny, on which Scottish Kings were crowned, to Westminster in England leading to the first war of Scottish Independence.

Whether it is because of her ongoing devotion to her husband, or whether it is through the torment of her son's reign as King leading to the two countries from which she and her husband were born going to war, it is said that the spirit of Lady Dervogilla is not yet at rest. Her ghost has been seen on many occasions walking within the walls of the now ruinous abbey and in particular ascending the central stairs. The figure is often described as wearing a long, flowing white or grey dress, leading to her being known as a grey, or white, Lady, a common type of ghost in Scotland associated with loss and heartbreak.

Queensberry House, Edinburgh

Towards the lower end of the Royal Mile in Edinburgh stands Queensberry House, once deemed one of the finest buildings in the city.

Queensberry House, Edinburgh

The property was initially constructed in 1667, with further additions being quickly added. Around 1686, it was sold to William Douglas, 1st Duke of Queensberry and became both his Edinburgh residence and, with its grand scale and fine finishings, a symbol of power.

The property remained the main Edinburgh residence for successive generations of the family until Edinburgh's

New Town began to be developed in the second half of the 18th century. Many of the wealthy city residents moved to this new, exclusive area including the Douglas family who left Queensberry House resulting in a complete reversal in its use.

It was initially rented then divided into smaller apartments to become more affordable for people to live in. By the start of the 19th century the house had been stripped of the fine finishings and sold to the Government, who converted it to a hospital. It was later used as army barracks, with additions being added to suit this purpose, before being returned to providing care facilities and refuge for the homeless. In 1948, it became a specialised until for the elderly, before finally closing in 1995. Two years later, in 1997, it returned to government hands and is now incorporated into the Holyrood Complex of the Scottish Government.

With its long and varied use, it would be fair to assume this historic property may have reports of a ghost or two, yet the tale of the haunting comes from a quite horrific incident that is said to have occurred in the property. After the death of William Douglas, the house was passed to his son, James, 2nd Duke of Queensberry. He went on to have a son of his own, who was said to be insane and violent to the level where he was kept locked up and guarded.

James would go on to become a deeply unpopular man in Scotland, due to his involvement in negotiating the Treaty of the Union, which brought the Scottish and English parliaments together under the 1707 Act of the Union. The unification was unpopular with large sections of the population in Scotland.

With general mistrust and fear of the changes it would

bring, public unrest and riots followed and, as a result, James would often have to take guards with him when leaving the security of Queensberry House and while travelling.

It is said that on one of these occasions, with the Duke away accompanied by his guards, that his son managed to escape from his confinement in the house. No one knows exactly what happened, yet it was later discovered that he had attacked one of the servants. He had then roasted the boy on a spit above an open fire and when he was found, it is claimed he was eating the servants cooked flesh.

Despite the property being stripped of its interior features around a century later, an early fireplace remains and many claim this was the one on which the servant was roasted. Since the incident, the agonising screams of the young man have been heard echoing around the house.

The Phantoms of Inveraray Castle

Inveraray Castle is, without a doubt, one of the most visually impressive castles in Scotland. Built for luxury, the current castle sits on the site of an earlier, fortified tower house, and gives little indication of the darker history this land we once witness to.

Inverarary Castle

The original castle was constructed around 1450 for Sir Colin Campbell of Glenorchy before being passed to his nephew, Colin, the 1st Earl of Argyll. It was believed to have been a traditional tower house with turrets on each corner, but little more is known about it. It is said to have been burned to the ground by the Marquis of Montrose who attacked the castle in 1644.

However, records indicate that the castle was found to have significant structural problems and was not demolished until the 18th century. It is possible these structural issues could have been as a result of a fire, although archaeological records of the foundations indicate these were found to have been constructed in haste and may account for the problems.

The new castle sits directly beside the site of the old castle and construction started in 1746 for the 3rd Duke of Argyll. When the castle was completed in 1785 by the 5th Duke, it had the basic quadrangular shape with turrets on the corners and a central square tower with Gothic features. A fire in 1877 caused considerable damage to the upper floor of the castle and when it was rebuilt, the additional attic floor and slate roof were added to the castle and a conical roof was added to each of the towers, completing the look of the castle.

The castle is said to have several connections with the paranormal, one being the ghost of a young woman who is thought to have been killed by the Jacobite forces, although nothing is really known about her or why she haunts the structure. The most frequently witnessed ghost relates to the Marquis of Montrose burning down the original castle. It is said that while the Duke of Argyll and the majority of inhabitants of the castle managed to escape a few, including the Duke's harpist, were left behind. They were captured by the attacking army, and the harpist was hanged on the castle grounds.

Since the construction of the new castle, there have been reports of the sound of harp music playing throughout the castle and, on occasion, a fleeting glimpse of the musician. This does off course raise the question of why anyone would haunt a building that was not constructed until after the time of their death, and there are several theories behind this.

Most reports of paranormal activity seem to be from the area of a room known as the MacArthur Room, in which there is a large, ornate bed said to have been salvaged from the old castle and brought to the new building. There is a local legend that the reason the harpist was left behind was as a punishment after he was caught watching the Lady of the Castle in her bedchamber through the keyhole, and it is possible this is the bed from that chamber.

The castle is also said to be haunted by a ghost that appears when the chief of the Clan Campbell is approaching death, but this particular apparition must be an impressive sight. It is claimed that a phantom galleon sails down Loch Fyne towards the castle, and when the ship reaches land, it continues to sail up to the castle as though it was still in the water.

Unusual as the ghost ship may seem, Inveraray lays claim to an even more unusual haunting, which is said to have taken place in July 1748, when a local physician and two colleagues witnessed a strange event while walking in the estate, which was also witnessed by two women who were walking in a different part of the estate. It is said that in the sky above the castle, they saw figures appear and a ghostly battle take place. All of them described it as though Highland soldiers were attacking a fort which appeared to be held by what they felt were French soldiers. Eventually the Highlanders were beaten back and had to retreat, leaving many of their dead and injured comrades as the French pursued them.

Several weeks later the news was received that there had been a battle at Fort Ticonderoga, in what is now New York State, USA. An army of fifteen thousand British and Colonial troops, led by General James Abercrombie, had attacked the fort, which was being held by the French.

Despite several attempts, the British and Colonial troops were unable to breach the fort's defensive walls and having suffered heavy casualties, they were forced to withdraw. Almost two thousand men lost their lives in the battle, almost five hundred of which were from the Scottish regiment, the Black Watch.

It appears what was witnessed above the castle was a type of crisis apparition, which is when someone who is not dead but is in great peril appears in front of a loved one to alert them to their crisis. However, why so many appeared at the same time and at the castle during their moment of peril remains a mystery.

The Ghosts of the House of Dun

The House of Dun is a very impressive Georgian Manor house situated a few miles from the town of Montrose on Scotland's east coast. While from the front it is easy to see the property for the manor house it is, from within the courtyard, surrounded by other buildings, it more gives the feeling of being a small community with an impressive row of houses rather than a single property. From here, it does not feel dissimilar to being in one of grand streets of Edinburgh.

The House of Dun

The two-storey house, with basement and attic level, was built in 1730 for the then Lord Dun, David Erskine. A tower house which dated back to the 14th century stood on the site previously, which had been the Erskine family home prior to the current mansion replacing it. The house remained in the Erskine family until it was left to the National Trust for Scotland in 1980. Although the property was being used as a hotel prior to being left to the National Trust, it had not suffered any significant changes as a result and it remains one of the most original Georgian properties in the country with its fine internal plasterwork remaining intact.

There have been reports from both staff and visitors of mysterious figures being seen on both the main staircase and in the library, although little is known about who these figures may be or why they still appear. It is probable that they are the residual energy of household members or staff from the property's history, continuing to be seen to be carrying out their daily duties as they did in life when the environmental conditions are correct for the replay.

The ghosts are not restricted to the house itself and there are also several figures which have been witnessed within the 370-hectare estate of the house. According to legend, centuries ago a knight had returned from fighting abroad to the surprise of the local community. He was told that a man had previously broken the news that the knight had been killed in battle, and so they were all surprised to learn that he was in fact alive and well.

But worse news was to be broken to him, which may explain the man's reason for the deception. After convincing everyone the knight had been killed, he approached his wife with a proposal and, distraught and believing herself to be a widow, she accepted and they became married.

Furious, the knight sought out the man and a fight ensued, in which he impaled his foe with his sword against a yew tree in the grounds of Dun House. There have since been reports of the phantom knight being seen standing close to an ancient Yew Tree, returning to the spot where he avenged the ultimate deception.

Another figure regularly seen is a headless man. He is reported to have been seen wandering around the many lanes which pass through and around the estate and although his identity is unknown, from his dress, many believe him to have been a huntsman leading to the belief that he suffered a tragic accident during a hunt (or may have been slaughtered by the ground-keepers if hunting illegally). As is common with other tales of headless phantoms, his spirit still roams seeking his missing head.

The final ghost of the grounds is normally heard rather than seen. A harpist is said to have met his death in a small, wooded area within the estate. At times, people walking through the grounds still hear his music playing through the trees.

The Roasted Commendator of Dunure Castle

Dunure Castle served as the stronghold for the Kennedy Family, the Earls of Cassils, a family that grew to become one of the most powerful in the country. As the influence of the family grew, so too did the castle with additional buildings being added to improve the living conditions, including a great hall, and a kitchen. A prison was also added.

The remains of Dunure Castle

After the 8th Earl died with no direct ancestors, ownership of the castle passed to Sir Thomas Kennedy of Culzean. With Sir Thomas already having a family residence at Culzean Castle, Dunure was surplus to requirement and decay soon set into the structure before the castle became a quarry for stones for the construction of local buildings. In the 1800s the importance of the castle was again recognised, and the castle was stabilised and now has the protected status of a Scheduled Monument.

The tale of the haunting comes from the time of the Reformation, when the castle was in the ownership of Gilbert Kennedy, the 4th Earl of Cassilis. The Reformation brought an opportunity for powerful families to take ownership of the lands being abandoned by the fleeing Catholic clergy. Gilbert Kennedy sought to take possession of the lands of Crossraguel Abbey but there was a problem with his plans. After the death of the last Abbot in 1564, a gentleman named Alan Stewart had been appointed by the King to oversee the Abbey and its lands. Despite Kennedy laying claim to it on the basis that the last Abbot was in fact Quintin Kennedy, a relative of Gilbert, Alan Stewart was unwilling to sign the land over to him.

After a five year dispute, Gilbert Kennedy decided to take matters into his own hands and invited Alan Stewart to the castle for discussions. Shortly after he arrived, Stewart was instead seized by a group of men put together by Kennedy. Curiously, the group included the Castle's cook and baker, yet their skills were needed for what was planned for the unfortunate Alan Stewart.

He was secured to the spit, and slowly roasted above the great fire, with great care to cause maximum discomfort without burning the skin so no evidence of his ordeal would be visible on his body. As is common with such stories, there are varying versions of the torturous treatment, including it only being his feet that were roasted, him being chained to a metal chimney and having parts of his body basted to concentrate the pain.

Whatever did happen behind the closed doors of the

Castle, the result was that Alan Stewart agreed to sign over the Abbey and its lands to Gilbert Kennedy. Although Alan Stewart survived his ordeal, the experience was to affect him for the rest of his life, and beyond. On the anniversary of his torture, ear-piercing screams are said to be heard from the castle prison, which are believed to be those of the spirit of Alan Stewart, the Roasted Commendator of Dunure Castle.

The Ghosts of Ardrossan Castle

Perched on a rocky cliff above the town of the same name, the ruins of Ardrossan Castle offer impressive views across the Ayrshire coast.

The ruin of Ardrossan Castle

Although the history relating to the earliest construction of the castle is unclear, it is widely believed the original castle was built for Simon de Morville during the mid part of the 12th century. By the early 12th century it was owned by the Barclay family before passing to the Eglinton family through marriage, and then the Montgomery family, again through marriage.

The castle was built very much as a defensive stronghold, although the Montgomeries did carry out extensive work during the 15th century to make it more comfortable to live in. When Oliver Cromwell invaded in

1650s, the family are said to have moved to one of their other properties which was more remote and provided better protection.

This led to Ardrossan Castle being first held and then destroyed by Cromwell's army, with the stone being used to help construct his citadel in Ayr. The decision was made not to rebuild the castle and it lay in ruins until the 19th century when some restoration work was carried out, although today the castle is considered to be in a dangerous condition.

Due to its location, the castle was always at risk of attack, hence being so heavily fortified. In 1292 the castle was held by the English until 1296, when William Wallace led an attack to retake it for the Scottish forces. Legend has it that Wallace's men set a small fire close to the castle, and when some English troops came to investigate they were slain. The Scots then dressed in the English soldiers uniforms and returned to the castle, where they were let in by the guards who believed they were those who had left to check the fire.

Once inside, they attacked the guards before opening the gates to allow Wallace's army into the castle. The English forces were slaughtered with the bodies being thrown into vaulted chamber. Some say that the survivors were also thrown into the same chamber, and left to die there. The chamber has since been known as Wallace's Larder.

There are several reports of hauntings connected to this incident, including the sighting of a tall, bearded figure walking silently through the castle ruins who many believe to be the spirit of William Wallace himself, returning to one of his greatest works of deception against the English, and also one of his most horrific acts if the living had been left to perish with the dead.

There is also a legend relating to the Devil connected to the castle. It is said that Sir Fergus Barclay was an impressive horseman, yet he had gained his skill not through practice but through a deal with the Devil who had granted him his abilities, in return for his soul. Sir Fergus; however' came up with a plan which got him out of the deal with the Devil, who in turn kicked the castle wall in a fit of rage, leaving a hoof mark in the stone.

Any satisfaction Sir Fergus had at beating the Devil was short lived. He is said to have gone on to murder his own wife before travelling to the Isle of Arran where he died soon after. His body was buried at the shoreline, and the sea washed it back to the coast at Ardrossan. His remains were recovered and reburied at the castle, yet his restless soul is still said to wander the castle.

<u>The Haunting of Castle Coeffin</u>

Little remains of Castle Coeffin on the island of Lismore, yet what does remain is striking. Visitors could easily be forgiven for thinking that the vegetation covered structure was part of an unusual natural rock formation, yet as you get closed it becomes clear it is the stone structure of the castle.

The finger-like ruins of Castle Coeffin

The islands had been held by the Vikings until their defeat by the Scots at the Battle of Largs in 1263. The Treaty of Perth in 1266 secured the islands for the Scots, and King Alexander III of Scotland returned Lismore to the Clan MacDougall. It is believed that the castle was built soon after for the MacDougall's of Lorn, although the exact date is not known. In fact there is little known about the history of the castle at all.

It is believed to have changed hands several times based on the lordship of the island of Lismore changing hands several times. By the time of the earliest written record for the castle in 1469, it was in the possession of the Campbells, with it being one of the items documented as being passed to Sir Colin Campbell of Glenorchy by his uncle.

With little more written about the castle in the records it is thought, although it remained in the ownership of the Campbell's until the 18th century, it was not used as a main residence for them and may not have even been used at all, allowing the property to fall into a state of disrepair and decay setting in. It is certain that by the 19th century the castle was a ruin and so it is possible it had been quarried for stones to build nearby structures.

The tale of the haunting comes from an older fortress that is said to have stood on the site, and from which the current castle took its name. It is told that this had been the stronghold of a Viking Prince named Caifen and that amongst those who lived there with him was his sister, Beothail. The young princess had fallen in love with a Viking warrior, yet was left heart broken when he was killed in battle in Norway. Grief-stricken, she too soon passed away and was buried close to the castle, yet her restless spirit began to be seen around the castle grounds.

She is said to have appeared to both her father and her brother and begged for her bones to be taken to Norway and buried with the remains of her true love. After several sightings, they did as was asked and had her remains exhumed, washed in the waters of the Holy Well to prepare and bless them for the sea journey ahead, and taken to Norway where she was buried in the same grave as her lover.

Any hope that this would end the haunting were however short lived, with her spirit continuing to be seen in the castle and again appearing to her brother and father to beg that her remains were taken to Norway. Close examination of her original grave revealed that one small bone had been left, and so it too was washed and transported to Norway, before being laid to rest with the remainder of her body.

After this it is said the ghost was no longer seen, however, more recent sightings seem to suggest this may not be the case. Visitors have reported catching a fleeting glimpse of a lonely figure walking through the ruins of the castle and some have reported anomalies appearing on photographs. Perhaps the spirit of Beothail feels compelled to still return to the place where she had both lived happily, and experienced extreme grief.

The Curse of Cardoness Castle

We end with a tale of a curse rather than a haunting, which is said to bring bad luck to all who live at Cardoness Castle. Although the tale of the curse dates back a long time, no one knows its origin. It is said to have been placed on the land rather than the castle itself, but unfortunately building the castle on the cursed land inflicted it on the occupants.

Cardoness Tower-house

Situated close to the rugged coastline of the South West of Scotland, a castle was believed to have been initially constructed for the Cardoness family, before ownership of the estate was transferred to the McCulloch family through marriage. A local legend about the events leading up to this marriage may be the origin for the belief in the curse.

It is said that the Laird of Cardoness and his wife had 9 children, all daughters. Infuriated that there was no male heir, he told his wife that if she did not give him a son he would drown her and their daughters in the loch on the estate. When she fell pregnant again it must have been a tense time, yet both the Laird and his wife rejoiced when a son was born.

To celebrate, the Laird decided to hold a gathering and with it being winter, he decided to take advantage of the frozen loch as a scenic location to host it. As the festivities were in full flow, the ice broke and all plunged to their death in the freezing water. One daughter had; however, remained in the castle and so survived.

When she went on to marry one of the McCulloch family, the castle and estate were transferred to her new husband. The McCulloch's were said to have been rivals to the Cardoness family, and so the estate landing in their hands was seen as punishment for the Laird for his terrible threat to his wife and family if he was not provided with an heir.

The current castle was constructed around 1470 by the McCullochs, and was designed as a defensive structure not just against invading forces, but due to ongoing disputes the McCulloch's held with their neighbours. It seems they had great ambitions to extend their estates, entering into several legal battles over land and even forcing one of their daughters to marry a local man described as being a 'natural idiot' in order to utilise his land.

The McCullochs did hold positions of significance which protected them to an extent, Alexander McCulloch was the keeper of the King's Falcon, yet he was also convicted on a couple of occasions for violence against his neighbour. Their crimes were not restricted to other families.

In 1501, following his father's death, Ninian McCulloch broke into a barn on the estate and stole a mix of around 1,500 animals from his mother. In 1530, the McCulloch's led a raid on the Isle of Man which would provide them with sufficient ill-gotten gains that they would return several more times to take more.

The endless battles and disputes were however expensive, and the family's fortune became drained to the level that the castle was lost. To add insult to injury, it was bought by John Gordon, one of the neighbouring families with whom the McCullochs had held so many disputes. Was history repeating itself with the castle and estate passing to a rival?

The McCullochs would not accept the loss however, and it is said that they attacked the home of the Gordons, dragging an elderly lady outside in the cold and throwing her into a dung heap. Godfrey McCulloch would go on to later shoot one of the Gordon family dead, leading to Godfrey being executed by beheading at the Maiden (a predecessor to the guillotine).

With misfortune once against falling on the owners of Cardoness, the castle was soon abandoned. It passed through the ownership of several other families, perhaps a sign that none wanted to stay there too long, before eventually falling into a state of disrepair. The ruins were put into state care and are currently maintained and operated by Historic Environment Scotland.

The castle does also have the tale of a traditional

haunting also, with the phantom figure of a woman seen walking through the building as though looking for something. Could this be the lonely figure of the wife of the Laird of Cardoness, still searching for her lost children?

About Scottish Paranormal

Scottish Paranormal is one of the oldest paranormal research teams in Scotland with a primary aim to document, and hopefully scientifically prove the existence of the paranormal.

Founded by Ryan O'Neill over 2 decades ago, we have developed a reputation not just for the quality of our work, but for our inclusivity and respect. We delve deep into the alleged hauntings across Scotland, and further afield, using both traditional and cutting edge techniques. We share our findings for all to view and while we will offer our thoughts, we leave it to the individual to form their own opinion on the potential causes.

Our approach has led us to have a large and loyal following, who appreciate our real and raw approach, and has resulted in us being given the opportunity to work with some of the most high profile locations in the country.

We also worked closely with the development of the TV show Spooked Scotland (Haunted Scotland in America) and Ryan was the main investigator for this series, along with the soon to be aired Spooked Ireland.

We welcome visitors from across the world to showcase our beautiful country, provide ghost tours, offer bespoke investigations and give talks to audiences and colleges to share our experiences.

We are now developing our own online series, carrying out intensive investigations at some of our favourite locations to try to get to the bottom of the hauntings.

To follow the work of the Scottish Paranormal team, and our wider Haunted Scotland organisation on social media please simply carry out a search for both Scottish Paranormal and our other organisation, Haunted Scotland.

Other paranormal related titles in the Scottish Paranormal range are as below:

The Unseen World: Afterlife Research
Witch Memorials of Scotland
Ghost Stories from the Historical Archives 1

www.ingramcontent.com/pod-product-compliance
Lightning Source LLC
Chambersburg PA
CBHW061002260726
48661CB00005B/2010